時代英

MW01225489

Fun with
English
Idioms

John • Ching Yee Smithback

FEDERAL PUBLICATIONS
Singapore • Kuala Lumpur • Hong Kong

First published in 1997 by
Federal Publications (S) Pte Ltd
A member of the Times Publishing Group
Times Centre, 1 New Industrial Road, Singapore 536196

ISBN 981 01 2310 8

Printed by Stamford Press Pte Ltd, Singapore

出版：
新加坡聯邦出版（新）私人有限公司

台灣地區發行總代理：
來來圖書有限公司
　地址：台北市羅斯福路三段 271 號 F4-1
　電話：(02)363-4265, 392-9765
　傳真：(02)362-5365

序 言

　　根據語言學家的研究所得：成語約占日常英語的三分之一。英語成語所包羅的範圍廣泛，有俚語、俗語、諺語、慣用語等。

　　成語是語言裡的精粹。成語來自人民的智慧，以及他們對生活的領悟，自然是多姿多彩；而且言簡意賅，短短幾個字就能夠把意思發揮得淋漓盡致。

　　由於成語在日常英語中擔任的角色頗為重要，莫說要充分掌握英語，就算與洋人作一般的溝通，或祇是想了解西洋電影的對白，都必須懂得相當份量的英語成語。

　　學習英語成語，說難不難；說易不易。以英語為母語的洋人，在牙牙學語時，便從父母、親朋、電影、電視等各種方面，逐漸學習和積累成語的知識。中國人則通常要到進入小學階段後，才對英語認真起來，而開始死記硬背成語。這時，他們可能會感到枯燥，又甚至發覺難以消化。

　　本書針對中國人學英語的困難，深入淺出，以風趣的文字，配上幽默的插圖，輕輕鬆鬆地引導你：怎樣活學活用英語成語，把日常英語表達得生動傳神。

目　錄

All the world and his wife • 一大群人 / 重要人物　1

And how! • 當然啦！/ 好極了！　2

At odd hours • 在非正常的時間裏　3

The bald facts • 顯而易見的事實　4

A battle/war of nerves • 策略鬥爭 / 心理戰　5

Be/Get lit (up)/Be lit up like a Christmas tree • 酩酊大醉　6

Be strapped • 現金不足 / 身無分文　7

Be tight-lipped • 守口如瓶　8

Between you and me and the bedpost/cat/gatepost • 這是你我之間的秘密　9

A (big) yawn • 無聊的人 / 事物　10

Break bread with someone • 與某人分享食物　11

Can't have one's cake and eat it too • 不能又要馬兒跑，又要馬兒不吃草　12

Carry the can • 替人承擔責任 / 代人受罪　13

Chew the rag • 談話 / 閒聊　14

Come down in buckets/Rain buckets • 傾盆大雨　15

Come to a head • 到了危及關頭　16

Crack the whip • 以嚴厲的態度來駕馭某人　17

The dawn chorus • 百鳥晨鳴　18

The devil has the best tunes • 價值不大的事情才最富有樂趣　19

Dip into one's pocket • 掏錢 / 慷慨解囊　20

Do a slow burn • 怒火愈來愈大　21

Do a stretch • 坐牢 / 服刑　22

Does not have a mean/selfish/jealous/angry, etc. bone in one's body • 并無卑鄙 / 自私 / 嫉妒 / 易怒等不好的品性　23

Don't darken my door • 不許登門 / 不准走近我家門口　24

Dressed like a jay • 穿上漂亮 / 色彩鮮艷的衣服　25

Drink like a camel • 痛飲一場 / 喝入大量的水　26

A financial/literary/etc. lion • 金融 / 文學等鉅子　27

The flip side • 唱片的第二面　28

Food that sticks to the ribs • 使人吃得飽而又有營養的食物　29

The gentle sex • 女性　30

Get/Find one's sea legs • 逐漸適應新工作 / 環境　31

Get/Give the (old) heave-ho • （遭）丟棄 / 開除　32

Get/Go through something like a dose of salts • 很快地完成某事　33

Get up (a head of) steam • 養精蓄銳 / 培養做某事的熱忱 34

Get up/Rise with the chickens • 清晨早起開始一天的生活 35

Give a jingle • 打電話 36

Give someone short change • 毫不憐憫 / 關心某人 37

Go to bed with the chickens • 入夜後便睡覺去 38

Go to hell in a basket/handbasket • （計劃、希望、機會，生命等）被毀滅 39

(Great) Balls of fire! • 啊呀！ / 天啊！ / 不得了！ 40

A ham actor • 演技拙劣的演員 41

Head for/Take to the hills • 匿藏起來 / 躲開某人 42

Have got to/Must hand it to someone • 賞識某人的某種優點 / 美德 43

Have swallowed the dictionary • 運用深奧、冗長的生僻字眼 44

Hide one's light under a bushel • 不露鋒芒 45

An honest broker • 意見中立的調停者 46

In from/out of the cold • 開始受到注意 / 重視 47

In/Into water • 處於 / 陷入困境中 48

In my book • 就我個人的意見 / 根據我的見解 49

In the air • 懸而未決 50

In/Out of tune • 與他人相處融洽 / 不和睦 / 適應 / 不適應環境 51

It/That figures • 這似乎是合理的 / 有可能的 / 正確的 52

Let the grass grow under one's feet • 浪費光陰 / 辦事極緩慢 53

Long in the tooth • 上了年紀 / 逐漸衰老 / 事物變得陳舊 54

Look like a drowned rat • 渾身濕透 55

Make a meal (out) of something • 小事化大 / 把事情複雜化 56

Make (the) feathers/fur fly • 引起激烈的爭執 / 毆鬥 57

The man in the moon • 吳下阿蒙 / 無知的人 58

Move/Shift mountains • 有才幹 / 能力 / 精力 / 信心去做一些重大的事情 59

Not worth a row of beans • 一文不值 / 毫無用處 60

On one's own hook • 獨自行事 61

On the fritz • 損壞 / 破爛 62

One could hear a pin drop • 極其寂靜 63

Out of the woods • 脫離困境 / 化險為夷 64

Out like a light • 昏迷 / 睡著 65

Past one's peak • 不如過去強健 / 有效率 / 能幹 66

A/Someone's place in the sun • 有利於工作與前途的地方 / 地位 / 環境 67

(As) Poor as Lazarus • 一貧如洗 68

Push up (the) daisies • 去世 69

Put something right/straight • 糾正錯誤 / 消除弊病 70

A (quick) turn of speed • 突然迸發出的速度 / 動力 71

The rain falls on the just and the unjust alike • 品行端正的人也必須承受生命中的風浪險阻 72

A red-letter day • 特別 / 重要的日子 73

Rest on one's oars • 苦幹了一段時間之後暫時歇一歇 74

Ride high • 取得成就 / 身於要位 75

Rise from the ashes • 自衰敗中振興起來 76

Run hot and cold • 態度 / 感情忽冷忽熱 77

Run like a train • 運作得很順暢 78

The sands (of time) are running out • 光陰似箭 79

Scotch the snake • 遏制麻煩 / 謠言 / 危險等 80

Seed money • 創業的本錢 81

Sign language • 手勢語 82

Sing in/out of tune • 唱得合調 / 走調 83

Smell a rat • 懷疑事情不妙 / 感覺事有可疑 84

(Something) Is someone's middle name • 某人的特質 / 個性 85

Spot on time • 準時得分秒不差 86

Spring for something • 做東道 87

Square something away • 打點某事 / 把某件事處理得井井有條 88

Squeeze something out of someone • 向某人施加壓力以獲取某物 89

Stand tall • 感到自豪 90

Strung up • 感到激動 / 不安 / 緊張 91

Sunday best • 在特別日子 / 隆重場合所穿的最漂亮的衣裳 92

Take a gander • 散步 / 閒逛 93

Take a gander at something/someone • 探頭 / 轉頭看某人 / 某事物 94

Take a leaf out of someone's book • 仿效某人 / 以某人作為典範 95

Take it from the top • 從頭開始 96

Take shape • 漸漸成形 / 變得具體化 / 使之實現 97

Talk a blue streak • 滔滔不絕地說話 98

Thanks a bunch • 非常感謝 99

That's all she wrote • 就此而已 / 已經完了 100

(As) Thin as a rail • 骨瘦如柴 101

Things that go bump in the night • 晚上聽見的異常聲音 102

Thrilled to the core • 感到欣喜萬分 103

Throw the baby out with the bath water • 整頓 / 革新事情時，竟連最重要的部分也給犧牲了 104

Tickle someone's funny bone • 逗某人發笑 105

Tie someone down • 限制某人活動的自由 106

(As) tight as a drum • 繃得很緊 107

Tight money • 難以借到手的錢 108

Time flies • 光陰似箭，日月如梭 109

(The) Times change • 時移世易 110

Tin Pan Alley • 流行音樂業 111

To beat the band • 喧噪地 / 猛烈地 / 驚人地 112

Too big for one's breeches/britches/pants/trousers • 自視過高 113

The tools of one's trade • 某人的行業裏所應用的裝備 / 工具 / 器具等 114

To the nth degree • 達到某種無 / 可衡量的程度 115

Turn one's stomach • 令人憤怒或反感 116

Turn someone off • 使某人發悶 / 厭煩 117

Under someone's heel • 在某人的勢力之下 / 被某人所控制 118

Up in the air (1) • 懸而未決 119

Up in the air (2) • 雀躍萬分 120

Walk the plank • 惹禍上身 / 遭遇不幸 121

The warp and woof (of something) • 某事物的基本要素 / 主要成份 122

Washed up • 一敗塗地 / 被毀滅 123

Watch every penny • 用錢的態度十分謹慎 124

Watering hole/place • 人們聚在一起喝酒、交際的酒吧 / 夜總會 125

Weigh something up • 衡量局勢 / 行動的成功率 126

The welcome mat is out • 歡迎某人隨時登門造訪 127

Well-heeled • 非常富有 128

Whoop it up • 狂歡作樂 129

Wipe the grin/smile off someone's face • 使某人不再過於自信 / 自滿 130

A witch hunt • 對異己份子的政治迫害 131

Work like a plowhorse/plough horse • 長時間地艱苦幹活 / 工作 132

Work up a storm • 以堅定的意志力勤奮地工作 133

Worn to a frazzle • 精疲力竭 / 心力交瘁 134

The year dot • 很久以前的某一刻 / 某個日子 135

You can bet your bottom dollar • 對某事非常肯定 / 極有把握 136

All The World And His Wife

"Come along, Erda," Mr Globus called. "We have been invited to a wonderful party, and **all the world and his wife** will be there." The idiom Mr Globus is using is a little old-fashioned. Yet, it is still used, particularly in Great Britain. "It refers to a large number of people, and especially to a large group of important people," Erda smiled.

"All the world and his wife" 是一句誇張的該諧語，不是指"全世界的人連同他的妻子"，而是借喻一大群人，尤其是指一群重要的人物。

And How!

"You have been very good children today," Mother said. "May I reward you with some ice cream?" Angela and Teddy were filled with joy. "**And how!**" Angela exclaimed. "**And how!**" Teddy shouted. As you might have guessed '**And how!**' does not mean NO. In fact, it means just the opposite. It is a strong and positive way of saying YES!

"And how!" 是一句感歎句，用以表示極肯定的答覆，其意思正如"當然啦！"，或者"好極了！"。

At Odd Hours

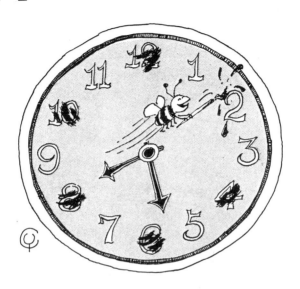

Helen does not go to work like other bees, so do not be surprised if you find her working **at odd hours**. **At odd hours** refers to times that are irregular or unusual. "Two o'clock in the morning might seem like a strange hour to be working," Helen yawned, "but I have trouble sleeping. That's why I'm often awake **at odd hours** doing my housework."

Odd 形容不是正規的或非固定的意思。"At odd hours"，意謂在非正常的時間裏。

The Bald Facts

"We are gathered here to discuss **the bald facts** of our recent business losses," the director said. In referring to **the bald facts**, the director does not mean he will be embarrassing the board members by talking about their lack of hair! "No, I will be discussing the plain and obvious facts with them," the director smiled. "That's what is meant by **the bald facts**."

Bald 一字除了形容禿頭，也是毫無掩飾的意思。 "The bald facts" 便解釋為顯而易見的事實。

A Battle/War Of Nerves

In a battle or a war, blood is shed and lives are lost. In **a battle/war of nerves** though, the only thing lost is a lot of sweat and maybe some sleep. That's because this expression refers to a tactical or psychological struggle between people, groups, or nations. "I think there is **a war of nerves** taking place in my waiting room today," Doctor Sigmund said.

在戰場上，傷亡與流血顯示了戰爭的殘酷；但在 "a battle/war of nerves" 裏，喪失掉的只是大量的汗水及睡眠。因為這句成語是指人、團體或國家之間的策略鬥爭或心理戰。

B^e /Get Lit (Up)/Be Lit Up Like A Christmas Tree

Rodney went to a party. "He went home **lit up like a Christmas tree**," someone said. That's true, for when I saw Rodney he **was** really **lit**! If you are wondering about the meaning of this, Rodney may be able to help you. "I was terribly foolish last night," he said, "and today I am ashamed of myself. To **get lit** or **be lit up like a Christmas tree** means to be very drunk," he confessed.

"Get lit" 或 "be lit up" 都是酩酊大醉之意。Christmas tree 是聖誕樹。"Be lit up like a Christmas tree"，是 "be lit up" 的誇張説法。

Be Strapped

In Winslow's business, all his customers **are strapped**. That is because Winslow is in the loan business, and when a person **is strapped** he is suffering from a lack of cash. In other words, he has little or no money. "Fear not," Winslow greeted a new customer. "Just sit down and fill out these forms. I will see to it that you will never again **be strapped**. Ha, Ha, Ha."

"Be strapped"，字面譯做"被皮帶捆住"，是借喻現金不足，或者身無分文。

Be Tight-Lipped

"There is something awfully funny going on in that house," LeCoeur's supervisor said. "Keep it under observation and report back to me," he said. A few days later, LeCoeur reported back. "I cannot tell you what is going on there," he said. "I promised those guys I would **be tight-lipped** about what I learned." To **be tight-lipped** is to be silent or to refuse to talk.

看字面意思，"be tight-lipped" 是 "緊閉雙唇"，這意指守口如瓶，對某事不發一言。

Between You And Me And The Bedpost/Cat/Gatepost

A married couple might say **between you and me and the bedpost**. Someone with a cat might say **between you and me and the cat**. Someone else chatting to a neighbor over the back fence might say **between you and me and the gatepost**. No matter how you choose to say this, it means "this is a secret, and it is just between you and me."

一對夫妻可能說 "between you and me and the bedpost"；養貓的人或會說 "between you and me and me and the cat"；與鄰居隔著圍牆傾談的人也許說 "between you and me and the gatepost"。總而言之，"between you and me" 和上述的說法，都解釋為 "這是你我之間的秘密"。

A (Big) Yawn

"I really and truly love my Granny, but the stories she tells are sometimes **a big yawn**," Suzie said. "I know," her little brother nodded. "In fact, the one she is telling us now was **a yawn** the last time she told it!" A story, a person, an event or an experience that is **a (big) yawn** is very boring. "I'll bet you a trip to the circus wouldn't be **a big yawn**," Granny smiled.

　　我們打呵欠 (yawn) 的時候，若不是疲倦的原故，便是對某事物感到無趣。"A (Big) yawn"，也就比喻使人感到極為無聊或無趣的人或事物，例如故事、事件、經歷等。

Break Bread With Someone

Unless a person uses this expression humorously, I think you will find that it is probably considered somewhat old-fashioned. It means to share food or a meal with someone. "It used to be awfully lonely in here," Albert said, "until I began inviting these little friends in to **break bread with me**. Now I'm happy, and all the birds seem pleased, too," he smiled.

　　麵包 (bread) 是西方人的主食之一，它是吃西餐時所不可缺少的。 "Break bread with someone"，意指與某人分享食物。

Can't Have One's Cake And Eat It Too

There are times when it just isn't possible to have, keep, do, or enjoy two things at the same time. Penelope, for example, can't spent her money and still save it for a holiday. She must remember that she **can't have her cake and eat it too**. "But nothing will stop me from taking a photo of my dessert and gazing at it while I'm eating it," Penelope smiled.

在人的一生裏，很少能夠做到兩全其美，或者從兩個對立的事件中兼收雙利。這便是 "can't have one's cake and eat it too" 所要揭示的道理。可比較 "又要馬兒跑，又要馬兒不吃草" 這句話。

Carry The Can

This idiom (it's one that is chiefly used in Britain) means to accept the blame or the responsibility for something that someone else has done – and usually they have misbehaved or done something wrong! "Everyone rushed home after the picnic and I was left **carrying the can** because I had to clean up the camping grounds by myself," Sidney complained.

　　昔日，在軍隊裏被委任 "carry the can" 的士兵，必須用罐子 (can) 替隊友載送啤酒。今天， "carry the can" 解釋為替他人承擔責任，或者代人受罪。

Chew The Rag

Long ago this idiom meant to argue. Later it meant to gossip. Today, though, when people **chew the rag** they are not arguing or gossiping: they are just having a nice little chat. "You aren't any fun to play with," Pedro complained. "You would rather sit there **chewing the rag**. That will not make anyone in the audience happy."

"Chew the rag"，從前解作爭論，後來形容說短道長，今天則是指談話或閒聊的意思。

Come Down In Buckets/ Rain Buckets

"Look at that!" Teddy cried. "It's **coming down in buckets**, and I didn't bring my umbrella today!" He and Angela continued walking home, though, and as you might have guessed they got very wet. That's because it **rained buckets**. When we say it **rains buckets**, or when the rain **comes down in buckets**, it rains heavily. "We got soaking wet!" Angela laughed.

Bucket 是水桶。"Come down in buckets" 或 "rain buckets" 都指雨下得很大，簡直像是傾注 而下。可比較中文成語裏的 "傾盆大雨"。

Come To A Head

The captain and the navigator of the S.S. Breakwater were arguing about the position of their ship at sea. Just as their argument **came to a head**, the ship sank. As the navigator swam to a nearby island, he smiled. "Ah, ha!," he said. "The captain was wrong and I was right!" When something **comes to a head** – an affair, an argument, a problem, a situation, etc. – it reaches a crisis point.

　　"Come to a head" 原指膿包成熟後，裏面形成一個膿頭；後也比喻事態、爭論、問題、處境等到了危急關頭。

Crack The Whip

When the circus came to their town, Chadwick and Timothy were asked to perform. Timothy was pleased to do so for it gave him an opportunity to finally **crack the whip**. "Stand there! Rise up! Don't move!" he called out to the frightened cat. "The reason I'm scared is because **crack the whip** means to exercise power or control over someone," Chadwick explained.

"Crack the whip"，指抽鞭子使發出噼啪的聲響。這是昔日奴隸主鞭撻奴隸，迫使他們服從自己的做法。今天給引申開來，比喻以嚴厲的態度來駕馭某人。

The Dawn Chorus

"It's five o'clock, time to get up and let everyone hear **the dawn chorus**," Gabby said. "When I count to three, let me hear your voices loud and clear. Are you ready? One, two...." A chorus is a group singing together, and Gabby is calling on his friends to start singing. **The dawn chorus** is the sound – some people would say noise! – of birds singing at dawn.

"The dawn chorus"，字面譯做"清晨大合唱"，是借喻黎明時鳥兒一齊發出的鳥聲或歌聲，即百鳥晨鳴。

The Devil Has The Best Tunes

About 200 years ago, a religious leader named John Wesley turned popular songs into church hymns. "Why should the devil have such good tunes and the church have such gloomy ones?" he asked someone. Today, someone doing unworthy things because it gives him pleasure might use this phrase humorously. "I know I watch too much television," Kurt said, "but I get bored studying. Besides, **the devil has the best tunes.**"

大約二百年前，英國有一名宗教領袖約翰・韋斯利曾嘗試以流行歌曲的曲調替聖詩譜樂。他問："憑什麼只有魔鬼才能擁有悅耳的曲調呢？"今天，當我們從事價值不大但卻富有樂趣的事情時，可以用 "the devil has the best tunes" 來自我解嘲。

Dip Into One's Pocket

Mr Winkle doesn't have much money but he never hesitates **dipping into his pocket** to help others. To **dip into one's pocket** means to spend or give money. "Mr Winkle is a very nice man," Buddy said. "He **dipped into his pocket** and gave me ten cents." "I enjoy being able to **dip into my pocket** to donate to worthy causes," Mr Winkle smiled. Later, Buddy was able to **dip into his pocket** to buy an ice cream cone.

"Dip into one's pocket" 意指：一、掏錢；二、慷慨解囊。這句成語的由來，大概因我們需要用錢時，就得伸手入口袋中掏出錢來。

Do A Slow Burn

Look out! Beware of Mr Grouch! I don't know what's bothering him today, but I can see he's **doing a slow burn**. "To **do a slow burn** is to slowly and gradually get angry," Grouch explained, "and I am **doing a slow burn** because my supervisor just informed me I would have to work overtime tonight!"

慢火燒的東西，其温度會逐漸地上升。故此，"do a slow burn" 也就借喻人的怒火愈來愈大。

Do A Stretch

Here is Albert **doing a stretch**. For all we know, Albert may be **doing a stretch** for many years to come. In informal speech, a 'stretch' is a jail or prison sentence, and to **do a stretch** is to spend time in jail or prison serving that sentence. "I have decided I will never be naughty again," Albert said.

俗語裏，stretch 是指徒刑；"do a stretch"，便是坐牢／服刑之意。

Does Not Have A Mean/ Selfish/Jealous/ Angry, Etc. Bone In One's Body

"Eddie is the most decent man I know," Betty said. "He **does not have a mean bone in his body**." In this idiom, 'bone' refers to an aspect of someone's personality. Depending on the person referred to, it could be any quality at all. "Bob **doesn't have a serious bone in his body.** He's always laughing." "Jill is nice to everyone. She **hasn't an unfriendly bone in her body**."

在 "does not have a mean/selfish/jealous/ angry, etc. bone in one's body" 裏，bone（骨）一字比擬人在某方面的個性。句中提出的 mean、selfish、jealous、angry 等，只是人的性格特徵的數個例子而已；整個句子也就解釋為某人并無卑鄙、自私、嫉妒或易怒等不好的品性。

Don't Darken My Door

"Hey! What are you doing there?" Edna cried. "Go away, and **don't darken my door** again!" What Edna is saying is that she does not want the person (in this case the house painter) to visit her or to come near her home again. This is nearly always said in anger. "She needn't worry. I **won't darken her door** anymore," the painter said to himself.

"Don't darken my door" 是一句口語，經常是在忿怒之下說出口的，告訴他人不許登門，或者不准走近我的家門口。

Dressed Like A Jay

Wally has been invited to a disco party after work. It's a very special party, so Wally has gone to work **dressed like a jay** today. As you can see, Wally's boss is not pleased about Wally's appearance. "The reason I am not happy is because when a person is **dressed like a jay**, he is dressed in his best – and often brightest – clothes," the boss said. "Wally's clothes are too bright for me!"

　　樫鳥 (jay) 是羽毛艷麗的鳥。所以，不論男女，若穿上漂亮，特別是色彩鮮艷的衣服時，便是 "dressed like a jay" 了。

Drink Like A Camel

Camels are famous for their ability to travel great distances through hot deserts without stopping for water. Before they begin a long journey, though, they consume great quantities of water, and it is from this interesting characteristic that we have the expression **drink like a camel**. "It's so terribly hot and I have been so thirsty that I've been **drinking like a camel** all afternoon," Alan said.

　　駱駝被稱為沙漠之舟，因為牠能夠在酷熱的沙漠裏長途跋涉而無需喝水。不過，在出發之前，牠必須喝入大量的水。"Drink like a camel" 便是從駱駝這種有趣的特點得來的成語，比喻痛飲一場，或者喝入大量的水。

26

A Financial/Literary/ Etc. Lion

A 'lion' is a person of great importance. We generally qualify these 'lions' by mentioning the profession in which they do well, as in these examples: "The newspaper referred to Mr Lee as one of the nation's top **financial lions**." "The success of Lester's new book transformed him from an unknown writer to a distinguished **literary lion**."

在動物的王國裏，獅子號稱萬獸之王。由此，一位顯要的人物就被喻為 "a lion"。這些 "lions" 在他們自己的行業裏，成就非凡，例如 "financial lion"，是金融鉅子; "literary lion"，是文壇名士。

The Flip Side

How often do you hear or read an expression, yet when you look in a dictionary you can't find it defined? Sometimes it is because the idiom or expression is very recent, as this one is. **The flip side** is the opposite or reverse side of a phonograph record. "I think you will enjoy hearing **the flip side** of this record," Stoney said.

　　唱片分為第一面與第二面。我們翻轉 (flip) 唱片的第一面時，便會看見它的第二面。故此，"the flip side" 也就指唱片的第二面。

Food That Sticks To The Ribs

Light snacks don't qualify as **food that sticks to the ribs**. To meet this description, a meal must be nourishing, and it must be a meal that makes you feel full. "My wife packs me a lunch of ham sandwiches and potato salad, with yogurt and pie for dessert," Paul grinned. "That's what I call **food that sticks to the ribs**!"

Rib 是肋骨。"Food that sticks to the ribs" 意指某些食物，但不是小吃或點心，而是能使人吃得飽，并且又有營養的一類食物。

The Gentle Sex

"I'll give you one guess to tell me who **the gentle sex** is**,**" Granny said as she boarded a bus. Looking at Mr Potter sitting on the ground, I suggested to Granny that men are **the gentle sex**. "No, you are wrong," she said. "It is women who are known as **the gentle sex**. That's because females are so sweet and gentle!" If that is true, I wonder what Mr Potter thinks of that?

在西方社會還未展開婦解運動之前，女性予人的印象是温柔、嫻靜，男士們便因此稱女性為 "the gentle sex"。

Get/Find One's Sea Legs

When a sailor gets accustomed to the motion of a ship at sea and is able to walk around comfortably, he **gets/finds his sea legs**. The same expression is used humorously by people who are adjusting to a new job or situation. "I have just been transferred to this department and I'm still learning my job. I haven't **found my sea legs** yet," our new supervisor joked.

　　當一名水手 "gets/finds his sea legs"，他是習慣了船隻在海上的顛簸，并且能夠安然地在甲板上走動。同樣的成語，若用在從事其他行業的人的身上，便是幽默地道出他們已逐漸適應新的工作或新的環境。

Get/Give The (Old) Heave-Ho

'Heave-ho' is a call used by sailors when lifting and throwing heavy objects around. From that, when something **gets** or **is given the (old) heave-ho**, it is thrown out. "I'm cleaning house and **giving the old heave-ho** to a lot of things I never use," Mary said. "The next time you're late for work, you're going to **get the old heave-ho**," the boss warned.

Heave-ho（啦喲）是水手在扯纜、起錨或起卸重物時發出的呼喊聲。"Give the old heave-ho"，就借喻開除某人或丟棄某物。"Get the old heave-ho" 便是被開除或遭丟棄的意思。

Get/Go Through Something Like A Dose Of Salts

In this expression, 'salts' refers to a type of medicine called mineral salts. The medicine is very fast-acting, and that's why **get/go through something like a dose of salts** means to finish or complete something quickly. "Teddy **goes through his morning exercises like a dose of salts**," Felix smiled.

瀉鹽 (salts) 是通腸胃的藥，其功效迅速。所以，"get/go through something like a dose of salts"，就比喻很快地完成某事。

Get Up (A Head Of) Steam

"I have been feeling so tired lately," Bertha said. "I haven't been able to **get up steam** to clean my house." Looking into her kitchen, she gasped. "Oh, dear. How will I ever **get up a head of steam** to do all those dishes?" To **get up (a head of) steam** means to brace enough energy to do something. "I can't even **get up steam** to go shopping," she added.

"Get up (a head of) steam" 意謂養精蓄銳，或者逐漸培養做某事的熱忱。這源出工業革命時代，藉蒸氣 (steam) 發動的機械，必須有足夠的蒸氣方可開動。

Get Up/Rise With The Chickens

You don't find chickens going to discos or staying up attending late-night parties! They are too sensible for things like that. They go to bed early so they can get up when the sun begins to rise. That is why **get up/rise with the chickens** means to wake up and start the day at an early hour of the morning. "Every day I **rise with the chickens**," Angela yawned.

雞隻(chicken)於破曉時分就醒來開始一天的活動。"Get up/rise with the chickens"，也就比喻人於清早起床，或者趕早起床來開始一天的生活。

Give A Jingle

JINGLE! JINGLE!

A jingle is a soft clinking sound. To some people, the sound of a ringing telephone must resemble a jingle because in colloquial English **give a jingle** means to call someone on the telephone. "I must **give** Angela **a jingle** to tell her I'm at home," Teddy said. "Guess who **gave** me **a jingle** at the office today?" Felix asked.

Jingle 是金屬相碰擊時發出的丁噹聲。有些人大概認為電話響聲就好像叮噹的聲音，所以俗語 "give a jingle"，就意指打電話（給某人）。

Give Someone Short Change

Merlin is accustomed to receiving somewhat larger sums of money when he begs from strangers. "But I don't have any small change!" Webster pleaded. "Too bad," Merlin said as he walked away, **giving** Webster **short change**. To **give someone short change** is to give him/her little or no attention. "And no sympathy either," Merlin said.

　　"Give someone short change"，意指對某人表示毫不憐憫或毫不關心。這源自給別人找回不足夠的零錢。

Go To Bed With The Chickens

There is an old proverb that says, 'early to bed and early to rise, makes a person healthy, wealthy and wise.' Angela certainly believes in that, for here she is, **going to bed with the chickens**. That is, she goes to bed early in the evening. "I feel more alert in the morning if I **go to bed with the chickens**," she explained.

"Go to bed with the chickens"，意指早睡。早睡的人像雞隻 (chickens) 一樣，入夜後便睡覺去了。

Go To Hell In A Basket/ Handbasket

This expression means that someone's plans, hopes, opportunities – or even his life – are ruined. "I bet on the wrong horse! My dreams of getting rich quick have **gone to hell in a handbasket**!" Sam cried. "I scratched my master's favorite chair," Chadwick sighed, "I think my hopes of getting fed today have **gone to hell in a basket**!"

Hell 是地獄。"Go to hell in a basket/ handbasket"，意指某人的計劃、希望、機會，甚至是生命都被毀滅了。

(G^reat) Balls Of Fire!

"**Balls of fire!**" Simon cried. "Look who our new
jailer is!" "Oh, **great balls of fire!**" Albert sighed.
"What did we do to deserve this?" **Balls of fire!** – or
the more emphatic cry of **great balls of fire!** – is
used to express amazement, surprise – or fear!
"**Balls of fire! I** quit!" the devil said. "You guys
aren't naughty enough for me!"

"Balls of fire!" 和語氣更強烈的 "great balls of
fire!"，都是驚歎語，用來表示恐懼、驚訝或詫
異的情緒。可比較中文的 "啊呀！"、"天
啊！" 或 "不得了！" 等。

A Ham Actor

Miss Josie Wimple is not happy. "Are you always this clumsy?" she asked the new actor. "You haven't even bothered to learn your lines in the play. You surely are **a ham actor**!" Anthony was terribly hurt for **a ham actor** is an inferior actor. It can also be someone who tries so hard to act that his/her performance looks exaggerated and foolish.

"A ham actor" 意指一位演技拙劣的演員，或者是因太賣力而使表演誇張到近乎慘不忍睹的藝人。

41

Head For/Take To The Hills

"Here comes that boat again! It's time to **head for the hills**!" Bighead cried. An old man sighed. "Even after all these years, it's hard to get used to **taking to the hills** every time that tourist ship comes here." No wonder he's tired, for '**head for/take to the hills**' means to get out of the way of something or someone. "I'm going to **take to the hills** where I can't be found for a hundred years," Bighead said.

"Head for/take to the hills"，解作匿藏起來或躲開某人。這大概來自舊日人們上山躲避敵人的追蹤。

Have Got To/Must Hand It To Someone

"I **have got to hand it to** Brighteyes. He is probably the most amazing dog in the world," Angela said. "The first thing he did after winning a trophy for intelligence was to give it to Teddy." When we say **have got to/must hand it to someone**, we are offering a compliment because we recognize someone's good features or qualities.

　　"Have got to/must hand it to someone" 是嘉許人的用語，表示賞識某人的某種優點或美德。

Have Swallowed The Dictionary

Some people say that Professor Oxbridge talks like a man who **has swallowed the dictionary**. What they mean is that he uses big words that aren't known to everyone. "I enjoy going to Professor Oxbridge's lectures, even though I don't always understand him. He's amazing to listen to. I wish I could talk like someone who **has swallowed the dictionary**."

Swallow 是吞嚥的意思。 Dictionary 是字典或辭典。 "Have swallowed the dictionary" 比喻運用深奧、冗長生僻的字眼。

Hide One's Light Under A Bushel

A bushel is a container used to hold a large measure of grain. This expression (it's from the Bible) means to be modest and to conceal one's talent or worthy qualities. "Why, Teddy! I didn't know you were such a clever painter," his teacher smiled. "You must show us more of your work and not **hide your light under a bushel** the way you have been doing!"

　　Bushel 是從前用來量穀米的籃子，它具有特定的容量。蒲式耳 (bushel) 這個容量單位即出於此。 "Hide one's light under a bushel" 源出《聖經》，意謂不露鋒芒，即是謙遜地斂藏自己的才幹、技藝或能力。

An Honest Broker

An honest broker is someone appointed to act as an agent in a legal, business or political situation. He is invited to offer an opinion when neutral advice is needed to settle a disagreement. He is called 'honest' because his opinions are neutral. "Rex Smith has been asked to serve as **an honest broker** to settle a dispute between the employees and the management."

　　"An honest broker"，直譯做"誠實的經紀人"，比喻受聘或被委任來解決法律、商業或政治等糾紛的一位調停者。他之所以被形容為honest，是因為他提供的意見是中立的。

In From/Out Of The Cold

A person **in from** or **out of the cold** is taken notice of and allowed to take part in an action or an event he had not previously been allowed to take part in. "I can't believe you have decided to let me **in from the cold**," the bear said. "I haven't needed your advice, but now that the hunting season has begun, it's time I brought you **out of the cold**," Nanook replied.

在這裏，cold（寒冷）比喻冷淡的態度；"in from/out of the cold"就指開始受到注意／重視，而且獲准加入以前不被允許參予的活動或事情。

In /Into Hot Water

Before visiting a foreign country, it is wise to learn something about the language, the culture, and the people of that nation. Jerome did none of those things, and that is how he got **into hot water** when he went to Japan. "I forgot to take my shoes off when I was invited into someone's home!" he exclaimed. "They were very, very upset about that." To be **in hot water** is to be in trouble.

當一個人 "in hot water" 時，他是處於困境中。至於 "get into hot water"，就解釋為陷入困境。

n My Book

"**In my book**, this library should be thoroughly cleaned and all the volumes inspected!" Professor Oxbridge frowned. "**In my book**, these books are infested with funny little worms!" What Professor Oxbridge means is that in his opinion the library should be cleaned. I know that because **in my book** means 'in my opinion', 'as far as I am concerned', or 'in my judgement'.

"In my book"，不是指"在我的書本裏"，而是解作"就我個人的意見"，或者"根據我的見解"。

In The Air

Things that are **in the air** have not happened yet. And the things most likely to be found **in the air** are hopes, plans, ideas, prospects, and projects. That is because when something is **in the air** no decision has been made. Its fate is unknown. "The meeting ended with the future of the building project **in the air**." "My hopes of getting promoted are **in the air**," Andrew said.

Air是空氣。"In the air"意指懸而未決。一般上，有可能 "in the air" 的事物有夢想、希望、計劃和方案等。

In Tune/Out Of Tune

"Matthew might be a great singer, but he's **out of tune** playing a guitar in my opera!" Helga complained. Helga isn't referring to the way Matthew plays his guitar, but where he is playing it. That's because **out of tune** (in this case) means something doesn't fit in. It does not suit the situation. "He'd be more **in tune** if he played his guitar at a rock concert," Helga explained.

"In tune" 本指唱歌或音樂和諧、不走調；引申開來，也解釋為與人相處融洽，或者可以適應環境。相反地， "out of tune" 便指與他人不和睦，或者不能適應環境。

It/That Figures

$$f(x) = f(a) + \frac{f^{[1]}(a)}{1!}(x-a) + \frac{f^{[2]}(a)}{2!}(x-a)^2 + \ldots$$

Winnie's child is intelligent, but if we said **that figures** we would not be referring to its remarkable ability to do sums. "No, we would not," Winnie smiled. "We would be saying 'that is likely', or 'that seems to be correct'." For example: "The sky is getting quite dark so **it figures** we will have rain." "Yes, **that figures**," Winnie's child answered.

"It/that figures" 不是演算數學題，而是解釋為"這是合理的"、"這是有可能的"，或者"那似乎是正確的"。

Let The Grass Grow Under One's Feet

Grandpa spends a lot of time sitting and thinking. Grandma sometimes accuses him of being lazy and **letting the grass grow under his feet**. If you waste time or are slow to get things done, you would be **letting the grass grow under your feet**. "I wish Grandpa was more energetic," Grandma said. "Personally, I like to get things done. I never **let the grass grow under my feet**."

"Let the grass grow under one's feet"，字面譯為"讓草在雙足下長出來"，是比喻浪費光陰，或者辦事極緩慢。

Long In The Tooth

As Dracula prepared to go out for the evening, he had a curious feeling that he was beginning to look **long in the tooth**. "Maybe I should return home early tonight," he said. "I'm beginning to feel a little **long in the tooth**." Things **long in the tooth** are old or aging. "Maybe all I need is a new suit. This one looks pretty **long in the tooth**," Dracula said as he gazed into a mirror.

"Long in the tooth" 形容：一、上了年紀或逐漸衰老；二、事物變得陳舊。

Look Like A Drowned Rat

The day was nice and Timothy thought he would take a voyage aboard a cruise ship. "That was my first big mistake," Timothy said later. "The ship sank and I walked ashore **looking like a drowned rat**!" If someone is said to be **looking like a drowned rat**, he/she is thoroughly wet. "The awful thing is that I'm not a rat! I'm a perfectly nice mouse!" Timothy cried.

Rat 是鼠；drowned 是溺斃。説一個人 "look like a drowned rat"，并沒有表示不好的意思，只是形容他渾身濕透而已。

Make A Meal (Out) Of Something

Chadwick takes time and goes to a lot of trouble to make the smallest event a special occasion. "I know. He surely **makes a meal of it**, doesn't he," someone said. That is, he makes something much more complicated than necessary. "I'm not a good cat around the house," Chadwick said. "If I chase a mouse, I always **make a meal out of that**, too."

Meal 是一餐或一頓飯。"Make a meal (out) of something"，意謂把小事化大，或者把事情複雜化。

56

Make (The) Feathers/ Fur Fly

When birds have a dispute, you can expect to see feathers flying in all directions. When animals have a serious fight, you can expect to see fur floating in the air. That's the idea behind this expression. **Make (the) feathers / fur fly** means to cause a fight or a fierce argument. "My wife said she'd **make feathers fly** if I didn't get home early tonight," Hanson said.

　　每當飛禽或動物在爭鬥時，鳥毛 (feathers) 和獸毛 (fur) 肯定是漫天飛揚，顯示牠們爭鬥得很激烈。由此，"make (the) feathers/fur fly" 也就比喻引起爭執或毆鬥。

The Man In The Moon

From earliest times, people have looked up at the moon and have sworn they can see the face of **a man in the moon**. As such claims do not bear scientific evidence, **the man in the moon** has come to represent someone who is ignorant or uninformed. "Please don't ask me any questions about history," Walter said. "I know as much about history as **the man in the moon**."

　　從遠古時代開始，人們早已相信有"月中人"之說，而且更斷言可以看見他的臉孔。由於這種說法沒有科學根據，"the man in the moon"就成為中國人所謂的"吳下阿蒙"，比喻一名無知或見識淺薄的人。

Move/Shift Mountains

People who are said to be able to **move/shift mountains** have the ability, the power, the faith or the energy to make big and important changes in their lives. "I am absolutely convinced that Wilbur and Orville have the ability to **move mountains**", Mrs Wright said. "My sons will **shift mountains** for they are very determined inventors."

Move 和 shift 都是移動之意。 Mountain 是山，能夠去 "move/shift mountains" 的人，是有才幹、能力、精力或信心去做一些重大的事情。

Not Worth A Row Of Beans

According to this idiom, a row of beans has no significance and is of little value. "I told Jerry I don't believe him. His promises are **not worth a row of beans**." "The dress I sent to the cleaners last week came back ruined. It's **not worth a row of beans** now," Helga sighed. "My old car is **not worth a row of beans**," Dickie said.

豆 (bean) 的價格很便宜，就算是一整籮的豆子也不會賣多少錢。"Not worth a row of beans"，也就指一文不值或毫無用處的意思。

On One's Own Hook

"It says here," Betty read, "that the object of fishing is to give a man a sense of pleasure and enjoyment being out of doors with nature." Her husband frowned. "I can do this without anyone's guidance," he spoke. "I prefer to do my fishing **on my own hook**." What he is saying is that he does not want help or advice. He wishes to do things independently. "That's what **on one's own hook** means," Betty smiled.

"On one's own hook" 形容獨自行事，完全不想要他人的協助或建議。這個成語也許出自單獨垂釣。

On The Fritz

"Hey, Jimmy!" Oliver called. "What does the word 'fritz' mean?" Jimmy scratched his head. "I don't know what 'fritz' means. Why do you ask?" "Because," Oliver said, "when a man dumped this refrigerator here I heard him say it was **on the fritz**." For Oliver and Jimmy's information, when something is **on the fritz** it is broken. This is usually said about machines and things like that.

"On the fritz" 雖然是很通俗的用語，但出處不詳，它形容物件損壞或破爛。

One Could Hear A Pin Drop

I don't think this is an expression you would ever think of using while riding a full bus to work, and I know you would not think of using it during the excitement of a football game. How do I know that? Because this idiom is only used in a situation of absolute silence. "Granny sat knitting, and it was so quiet in the room **one could hear a pin drop**."

"One could hear a pin drop"，形容極其寂靜，就連一根針掉在地上的聲音也都能夠聽到。

Out Of The Woods

"Trouble, trouble, and more troubles," Jerome sighed. "Just as I solve one problem, I am faced with another. Will I ever get **out of the woods** and be at peace?" The 'woods' Jerome is complaining about stands for trouble and difficulties. It could even refer to danger! "If I think hard and apply myself to these problems, I might be **out of the woods** in a week," Jerome said.

"Out of the woods" 原指人在森林 (woods) 裏迷途，但幸而找到方向安全地走出森林。這個成語後來引申為脫離困境，或者化險為夷。

Out Like A Light

"There," Henry smiled as he turned out the lamps.
"They are **out like a light** now." Henry is making a
joke, for to be **out like a light** is to be asleep or
unconscious. "The boxer fell to the floor. It was
apparent he was **out like a light**." (Unconscious). "I
was so tired that the moment I got into bed I went
out like a light," Henry said. (Asleep).

　"Out like a light"，直譯為"像燈一樣地熄掉
了"，用以比喻人昏迷過去，或者睡着了。

Past One's Peak

Pete used to be a fantastic athlete. "These days, some people say I'm **past my peak**," he said. When someone is **past his peak**, he is no longer as strong, efficient or able as he once was. It's usually because he is older and less capable. "But I can still climb mountains, and I'm going to climb this one to prove I'm not entirely **past my peak**," Pete boasted.

Peak（山峯）象徵健康或事業等的高峯。
當一個人 "past his peak" 時，便不如過去強健、
有效率或能幹；這是因為他年紀漸大而辦事能力
減低的原故。

A /Someone's Place In The Sun

"At last!" Ken cried. "After all these years I have found **my place in the sun**!" Ken has not moved to a warm and sunny tropical island: he is simply saying that he has reached a place or a position that is favorable to him, his work, or his future. "It has taken me a long time, but I have finally achieved **a place in the sun**," Ken said.

　　如果我們要尋找 "a/one's place in the sun"，是不用前往熱帶地區的，因為它是指一個有利於工作與前途的地方、地位或環境。

(Aˢ) Poor As Lazarus

"In the Bible (Luke 16)," Buddy explained, "you will find a story about a poor beggar named Lazarus. He wasn't just poor, he was frightfully poor," Buddy continued. "It is from that story that we have this expression, so to be **(as) poor as Lazarus** is to be really and truly poor. By the way, in case you haven't noticed, I'm **poor as Lazarus** myself," he said.

　　根據《聖經》的記載，Lazarus 是一個極為貧窮的乞丐。由此，"(as) poor as Lazarus" 就比喻一貧如洗。

Push Up (The) Daisies

A daisy is a flower. Why this certain flower is featured in this colloquial expression has never been made clear. That doesn't matter, though, as long as we remember that when someone is said to be **pushing up (the) daisies** he is no longer alive. He is dead. "Poor Freddie. He refused to quit smoking and today he's in the cemetery **pushing up daisies**."

　　Daisy（雛菊）是一種小野花，它不僅蔓生遍野，也經常生長在墓地周圍一帶。這源自美國的 "push up (the) daisies"，是一句詼諧的俚語，意指去世。

Put Something Right/ Straight

"Wow! That was in serious danger of falling!" Willard said. "Whoever built that tower didn't follow instructions! But I have **put it right**." To **put something right/straight** is to do what Willard did. That is, to correct a mistake, change a faulty situation, or to remedy a wrong. "In years to come, people all over the world will say it was Willard Smith who **put things straight** at Pisa," Willard grinned.

Right 形容對的; straight 形容正確的。 "Put something right/straight" ,解釋為糾正錯誤 (的事情、行為、局面等) ,或者消除弊病。

A (Quick) Turn Of Speed

For someone who has just learned how to ski, Rex sure has **a turn of speed**! I witnessed him the other day when I saw him racing down a mountain. He was about halfway down when a great big bear crossed his path! With **a quick turn of speed**, Rex zipped out of danger. "This idiom refers to a sudden blast of speed or energy," Rex said.

"A (quick) turn of speed"，直譯為 "一（急）轉的速度"，比喻突然迸發出的速度或動力。

The Rain Falls On The Just And The Unjust Alike

The saying that **the rain falls on the just and the unjust alike** is from the Bible. It states that no matter how just (good) or unjust (bad) a person is, he must still face the everyday problems that confront us all. In other words, being moral and righteous does not necessarily protect a person from the distressing hardships of life.

"The rain falls on the just and the unjust alike" 源自《聖經》，意思是不管是好人還是惡人，都必須面對生活中的各種問題。換句話說，品行端正的人，也必須承受生命中的風浪險阻。

A Red-Letter Day

In days of old, calendars used to have all the holy days marked in red so that they could be easily seen and remembered. In time, that led to this expression, and it now refers to any special or important day. "The 17th of March will always be **a red-letter day** for me," John smiled. "That's a very special day, for that's the day I met my wife."

在從前的西方社會裏，日曆上所有的宗教節日都以紅色作為標記，使它們顯眼及便於記憶。"A red-letter day" 便由此得來，比喻一個特別或重要的日子。

Rest On One's Oars

It seems to me that Teddy is **resting on his oars** today! This idiom (it's from the sport of rowing) means to take a long rest after a period of hard work. "This has been a difficult week for me," Teddy explained. "Thank goodness my examinations are over so I can **rest on my oars** and do nothing," he smiled.

Oar 是船槳。"Rest on one's oars" 源出划船競賽，意思是苦幹了一段時間之後，暫時歇一歇。

Ride High

Marcel has certainly been **riding high** since he won a promotion! At the moment he seems to have everything he has ever wanted – including a nice big camel! "I feel I have been successful. That's why I am **riding high** today," Marcel smiled. When someone **rides high**, he or she has achieved success and reached a position of social or financial importance.

　　昔日，馬是一種身份的象徵。貧苦大眾是負擔不起一頭馬的，而僕人又不准騎馬，於是那些高高在上騎馬代步的人，都是有身份、有地位或富裕的人。由此，"ride high"就引申為取得成就，并且身居要位。

Rise From The Ashes

The phoenix is a mythical bird that is said to live for 500 years. At the end of that time, it sets itself on fire and then it is destroyed – only to be reborn to live for another 500 years. That has given us **rise from the ashes**, an expression that means to rise from ruins to begin again. "I must congratulate Susan. After failing her examinations last year, she **rose from the ashes** to pass her studies with honors!"

　　鳳凰是古代傳說中的鳥，其壽命長達五百年。相傳此鳥每五百年自焚後從灰燼中再生。"Rise from the ashes" 便由此得來，解作自衰敗中振興起來。

Run Hot And Cold

"You sure confuse me," Fiona frowned. "One day you are in favor of having a picnic, and the next day you are opposed to it! Your interest in picnics seems to **run hot and cold**!" I think Fiona has a reason to be puzzled because when someone **runs hot and cold** his attitude or feeling about something (or someone) is constantly changing. "To be honest, my interest in you **runs hot and cold**," Peter explained.

Hot 是熱; cold 是冷。 "Run hot and cold" 意指對人或事物的態度或者感情忽冷忽熱，經常轉變。

Run Like A Train

Anything mechanical – a machine, an engine, a watch, a motor – that **runs like a train** runs or operates smoothly and well. "The garage mechanic repaired my car. It's **running like a train** again." "It looks like an elephant stepped on your watch," the jeweler said, "but leave it with me and I'll have it **running like a train** soon."

昔日，利用蒸氣開動的火車是很有效率的。故此，任何機械，例如一部機器、一個引擎、一隻手錶等，若是運作得很順暢，便是 "run like a train" 了。

The Sands (Of Time) Are Running Out

To say **the sands (of time) are running out** is to say that time is passing by quickly. It implies that if you have something to do, you should hurry and do it without delay. Here is an example of that: "If you hope to pass your examinations, you have little time in which to study. **The sands are** quickly **running out**," Charles warned.

"The sands (of time) are running out" 是指光陰似箭，時間流逝得很快，應該好好地把握。這出自計時的沙漏，上部份的沙 (sands) 從中間的小孔滲出，流入下部份，直至滲完，那就相當於若干時間的消逝。

Scotch The Snake

In this expression (it's from Shakespeare's play, *Macbeth*) the word 'scotch' means to make something harmless or useless. The word 'snake' is a metaphor for trouble or danger. Because false stories can be troublesome and sometimes dangerous, **scotch the snake** refers to stopping gossip or a rumor. "It's been reported that I am resigning," Mitchell said. "I want to **scotch the snake** now by telling you that is not true."

"Scotch the snake" 來自莎士比亞的《麥克白》一劇，字面譯做"把蛇打傷使牠不能為害"，是借喻把麻煩、謠言或危險等遏制下來。

Seed Money

A few years ago Mortimer visited his friendly bank manager to discuss the possibility of getting a loan. "I would like to borrow **seed money** to buy a great big farm," he explained. The bank manager smiled and gave Mortimer all the money he wanted. That's why Mortimer is now a successful farmer. "**Seed money** is the capital used to start a new business," Mortimer explained.

種子 (seed) 是植物的根源，發芽萌長後，便開枝散葉。所以，"seed money" 也就比喻為創業的本錢。

Sign Language

To people who are deaf, **sign language** is a system of hand gestures used for communication. **Sign language** is also a term used to describe the way people use their hands and arms to form signs or signals when communicating, particularly by people who speak different languages. "Isn't this a beautiful jar?" Gerald grinned. "I bought it in Mexico using **sign language**."

　　"Sign language" 原指聾啞人士相互溝通的手語系統，引申開來，便是我們與他人，尤其是指和語言不通者，互相傳達信息的手勢語。

Sing In/Out Of Tune

Try as he might, Pedro finds it impossible to **sing in tune**. "No matter how long I practice, all my sounds come out funny. I am always **singing out of tune**," Pedro said. To **sing in tune** is to sing the notes of a song right and in the correct musical pitch. Pedro can't do that. That's why we say Pedro **sings out of tune**.

Tune 是曲調。"Sing in tune" 解作唱歌唱得合調;"sing out of tune",則指唱走調。

Smell A Rat

"Isn't that strange. I haven't seen or heard the cat all day," Henrietta said as she sat before her mirror preparing to go out. "I know he's near, though, and I know he knows where I am. So I must be careful for I **smell a rat**!" To say that you **smell a rat** means you are suspicious or you have a strong feeling that something is wrong. "I hate being accused of being a rat!" the cat muttered to himself.

鼠 (rat) 是惹人討厭的動物，所以與鼠有關的英語成語，大多數含有貶義。 "Smell a rat" 也就比喻懷疑事情不妙，或者感覺事有可疑。

(**S**omething) Is Someone's Middle Name

If you are cautious – as John Doe is – you might say that **caution is your middle name**. If you are honest, someone might say that **honesty is your middle name**. Almost any word can be inserted in this expression, for when we say (**something**) **is someone's middle name** we are stressing an outstanding feature of his/her character or personality.

西方人一般上都擁有中間名字 (middle name)，例如 John Bell Smithback。然而成語裏的 "(something) is someone's middle name" 就另有意義，它指某人的特質或個性，例如 caution（謹慎）、honesty（誠實）等。

Spot On Time

"It has been a long, long winter," Irma smiled, "but spring has finally arrived and it is **spot on time**." To be **spot on time** means to be exactly on time – and that does not mean one second early or one second late. "Of course, when I said spring was **spot on time** I meant it was exactly on time according to the calendar," Irma explained. "Naturally, you would not expect spring in January!"

Spot on 是正中目標的意思。"Spot on time"是形容準時，就連分秒都絲毫不差。

Spring For Something

When the waiter brought the check to our dining table, Josh jumped up. "I feel rich! I'll **spring for the entire dinner** tonight," he smiled. No one argued with Josh about that because to **spring for something** is to treat a person by paying his share of a bill. "I'll let you **spring for my meal** the next time we get together to have dinner," Jose said.

"Spring for something"，指做東道，例如請某人喝茶、吃飯、看電影等。

Square Something Away

Ahmed seems to have a problem getting his performing snakes **squared away**. "I know that my pets are more or less round," he said, "but if I **square them away** properly, I can fit them all into one basket." That explains the care Ahmed is taking with his snakes. "Yes," he said, "because to **square something away** means to attend to a matter or to put it in order. So I'm just putting my snakes in order."

Square 指安置妥當。"Square something away" 就解作打點某件事,或者把某件事處理得井井有條。

Squeeze Something Out Of Someone

This expression means to apply pressure to someone in order to obtain something from him. The pressure might be mild (like asking him a lot of questions), or it might be severe (such as making threats). "The police are questioning the criminals in an attempt to squeeze some information from them. I understand they were **squeezing money out of the neighborhood shopkeepers**."

Squeeze 是壓榨之意。"Squeeze something out of someone"，意思是向某人施加壓力以獲取某物，如問大量的問題，或發出恐嚇。

Stand Tall

When people speak of **standing tall**, they mean that they are feeling proud. "You can **stand tall** knowing you have performed well. Each of you will be very pleased with your achievements," Professor Oxbridge told the students. "That's great!" Teddy exclaimed. "I thought I had failed the examination. I'm glad I can smile and **stand tall**!"

"Stand tall" 是源自美國的一句用語，解釋為感到自豪，尤其是指因滿意於本身的成就而以此自豪。

Strung Up

It's not often that George gets **strung up**. "But I'm a normal man with normal emotions, so if things don't work out as I'd like, why shouldn't I get **strung up**?" he asked. "If you had been here since dawn and you had no fish to show for your efforts, you'd probably be **strung up**, too!" George said. He's probably right – and by the way, to be **strung up** is to be tense, nervous or upset.

Strung（string 的過去分詞）意指被拉扯得緊。"Strung up"，形容感到激動、不安或緊張。

Sunday Best

Teddy and Uncle Felix are going to church. As you may have noticed, they are all dressed up in their **Sunday best**. "What would happen if we didn't wear our **Sunday best**?" Teddy asked. "Nothing would happen," Uncle Felix answered, "but it's nice to look nice, don't you agree?" I don't think anyone would disagree with that, especially since **Sunday best** refers to one's very best clothes worn on special occasions.

　　星期天是基督徒做禮拜的日子，為了表示尊重，他們皆穿上最體面的衣裳，稱之為 "Sunday best"。引申開來後，"Sunday best" 也就指在特別的日子或隆重的場合所穿的最漂亮的衣裳。

92

Take A Gander

A gander is a male goose. Apparently they have a habit of wandering about slowly for when a person **takes a gander** he takes a slow walk or a peaceful stroll. "I have to go shopping this afternoon," Angela's mother said as she left the house. "Why don't you **take a gander** in the park while I'm out?" Angela did just that – but I don't think that's what her mother wanted her to do!

　　Gander指雄鵝。雄鵝大概有到處漫遊、徘徊的習性，所以才出現"take a gander"這一成語，意謂散步或閒逛。

Take A Gander At Something/Someone

As we have just learned, a gander is a male goose. From the fact that geese have long necks, when a person bends or turns his neck to look at something he **takes a gander at** it. "Hey, **take a gander at** Angela!" her mother exclaimed when she returned home from shopping. "She's in the garden **taking a gander at** the new storybook I just bought her."

鵝有長長的頸項。由此，"take a gander at something/someone" 就比喻探頭，或者轉頭看某事物或某人。

Take A Leaf Out Of Someone's Book

In this idiom, a leaf is a page from an imaginary book in which someone had written down all his actions and deeds. To **take a leaf out of someone's book** is to copy or use one or more of those actions or deeds. "Wallace has **taken a leaf out of his brother's book** and has decided that he, too, will go to university to study science."

"Take a leaf out of someone's book"，直譯做 "從某人的書中摘下一頁來"。這只是一本想像 的書，記載着某人的行為事跡。故此，以上的 成語便借喻仿效某人，或者以某人作為典範。

Take It From The Top

"Oh, no! That's wrong" the chief engineer exclaimed as Ahrmad was about to put in place the final stone of a new construction in the desert. "I must insist that you **take it from the top** and build that thing all over again," he declared. To **take it from the top** means to begin again, to start all over. "Some people have no understanding of art," Ahrmad mumbled as he dismantled the structure.

"Take it from the top"，是指從頭開始的意思。這源自樂團的排練，指揮要求團員由某樂章的開始部份重新演奏。

Take Shape

From this illustration, it appears that Jackson has been lifting weights with only one arm! Still, that's not bad for it looks like his muscle-building program is starting to **take shape**. When something **takes shape** – an idea or a plan, for instance – it begins to take form and the final results seem about to be fulfilled. "My dream to have a body like Superman's is starting to **take shape**," Jackson said.

　　Shape 解作形狀，亦指具體化或實現。當某事物，如物體、概念、主意、計劃等 "take shape" 時，便是漸漸成形、變得具體化或使之實現。

Talk A Blue Streak

When Billy's mother complained that he always **talked a blue streak** while she was on the telephone trying to listen to someone, Billy rushed out to buy a copy of this book. Turning to Page 98, he read this statement: "To **talk a blue streak** means to talk on and on – and usually to talk quite fast." From that moment on, Billy remained very quiet whenever his mother was on the telephone. I think Billy is a smart little boy!

A blue streak 直譯為 "一道藍色的閃電", 比作迅速地行動。 "Talk a blue streak", 就借喻滔滔不絕地說話, 而且通常是說得又急又快。

Thanks A Bunch

"Oh, my! What a lovely bunch of flowers!" Beth cried with delight. "They are absolutely beautiful! **Thanks a bunch**, Fred!" Fred was pleased for he knows that **'thanks a bunch'** is a special way of saying thank you very, very much. "It's a colloquial expression," Fred said, "and I wish to say **thanks a bunch** to all the readers who have stopped here to learn this idiom."

　　在西方社會裏，送束(bunch)鮮花來表達謝意，是很普遍的做法。所以，"thanks a bunch"這句通俗語，用來表示非常感謝。

That's All She Wrote

This North American expression means 'that is all there is,' or 'that is the end; there is no more/ nothing more.' Here's an example or two: "The play is over, **that's all she wrote**," Peter said as the theater lights came on. "It's closing time at the park, **that's all she wrote**," the attendant said as he prepared to close the gate. "**That's all she wrote**, we're out of gas," Ned said as the car rolled to a stop.

Wrote（write 的過去式）是書寫的意思。"That's all she wrote" 產生於第二次世界大戰期間，某位士兵的女朋友給他寫了一封信，表示雙方的愛情已經結束。由此，這一北美用語便解釋為"就此而已"，或者"已經完了"。

(A^s) Thin As A Rail

I don't think Robert's model is going to be happy when she sees the picture he has painted! In it, she is **as thin as a rail**! "But she is **thin as a rail**," Robert defended himself. "To tell the truth, to be **thin as a rail** is to be skinny," the model said. "And a rail is a kind of post used to build a fence."

用來築籬笆的欄杆 (rail) 一般上是用木或金屬製造的,它的形狀瘦長。故此, "(as) thin as a rail" 就比喻人非常瘦削,簡直骨瘦如柴。

Things That Go Bump In The Night

Teddy is spending the week at Grandmother's house – and it's really scary at night! "I haven't been able to sleep!" Teddy whispered. "I hear noises, and sometimes it sounds like someone walking around. I wonder, is that Grandmother? What's that noise?" Teddy is hearing **things that go bump in the night**. These are unusual sounds or noises heard at night when a house is quiet. Because everyone else is sleeping, they can be frightening!

在夜闌人靜時，聽到物件無端端地碰撞 (bump) 所發出的聲響，難免會使人感到不安。 "Things that go bump in the night"，也就比喻在 晚上聽見的異常聲音。

Thrilled To The Core

The core of an apple is its central part. It's the part with the seeds. We aren't constructed in the same way as apples, of course, so when a person speaks of his core he means his deep, innermost feelings. Therefore, to be **thrilled to the core** is to be deeply pleased. "I was **thrilled to the core** to be invited to Sally's party." "I'd be **thrilled to the core** if you would attend the dance with me," Barbara said.

　　蘋果的果心稱為 core。當某人談及他的 core 時，其實是指他內心深處的感情。所以，"thrilled to the core"，便形容感到欣喜萬分。

Throw The Baby Out With The Bath Water

When reorganizing or changing something, be careful! Don't be so eager to get rid of the old or the bad that you end up losing the most essential part! It might be the most important part, and you could be **throwing the baby out with the bath water**! Here's Bradford using the expression: "I restructured my office staff, but in doing so I **threw the baby out with the bath water** for all my key employees quit!"

　　替嬰兒洗澡後，當然不會把他連同污水一起倒掉。"Throw the baby out with the bath water" 只是借喻整頓或革新事情時，因急於去劣除舊，竟連最基本或最重要的部份也給犧牲了。

Tickle Someone's Funny Bone

"I could swear I heard someone giggle," Yarda gulped. "I wonder if I'm doing something to **tickle this creature's funny bone**?" I think Yarda did hear someone giggle, but he would be wasting his time searching for this particular bone because to **tickle someone's funny bone** is an idiom. It means to amuse someone, to make him laugh. "Hear that? I'm sure I heard someone giggling!" Yarda whispered.

Funny bone 是肘部尺骨端，受觸時會產生發麻的感覺。"Tickle someone's funny bone"，就是我們所謂的"搔着某人的癢處"，也即是逗某人發笑的意思。

Tie Someone Down

"Your school holidays are over. School begins tomorrow, and I know that will **tie you down**," Mother smiled. "Gee," Angela said, "aren't we too young to be **tied down**? I thought only big people with important responsibilities got **tied down**!" To **tie someone down** is to restrict his freedom of action or his movement. "I'm beginning to think we will be **tied down** until we're old maids," Angela moaned.

把人捆綁起來，是要使他動彈不得。所以，"tie someone down" 比喻限制某人活動的自由。

(Aˢ) Tight As A Drum

"Jump, Finnigan, jump!" the firemen shouted.
Finnigan did jump – and he bounced right out of
their net! "Your net is **tight as a drum**," Finnigan
complained. "We are truly sorry," the firemen said.
When something is **(as) tight as a drum** it is very,
very tight. This comes from the fact that the
playing surface of a musician's drum must be very
tight. "I'll never jump into your net again,"
Finnigan said.

　　樂鼓 (drum) 的鼓面必須非常緊，才能敲出
理想的音響效果。由此，"(as) tight as a drum" 形
容繃得很緊，好像鼓面一樣。

Tight Money

Sometimes it is easy to borrow money from lending institutions – and sometimes it is difficult. When it is difficult to borrow, money is said to be tight, and **tight money** simply refers to money that is hard to borrow. This is usually due to a plan or a policy of the banks or the government. "The treasury department declared that **tight money** was the only way to bring down inflation."

向貸款機構借錢，時易時難。難以借到手的錢稱為 "tight money"。這種情況的產生，一般上是由於銀行或政府當時實施的某種政策所致。

Time Flies

Agatha received a new broom for Christmas. "Wow, these super new high tech models are so efficient my work takes no time at all now," she said. "And it's remarkable how **time flies** when a person is having fun!" she giggled. When we say **time flies** we are saying time goes by rapidly. "It goes by so fast we don't even notice it has gone," Agatha added.

　　"Time flies" 指時間流逝之快，讓人全然不覺；正是"光陰似箭，日月如梭"。

(T**he**) Times Change

WHERE DID THE PEOPLE GO?

Few things in this world stay the same. Things
that once seemed important give way as new
things become meaningful and old ideas are put
aside and forgotten. That is why it's not unusual
for us to say **(the) times change**. What we mean is
that things do not remain the same. "The young
aren't content to live as we did," Grandmother
sighed. "**Times change**, and they want new cars
and bigger homes. Things don't seem the same
anymore."

世事很少會恆久不變。新事物取代昔日曾
受重視的舊事物,古老的思想亦被淘汰。我們
經常說 "(the) times change" ,也許就是這個緣
故。

Tin Pan Alley

Years ago, an area in New York City housing the offices of composers and publishers of popular music was referred to as **Tin Pan Alley**. That was probably because some people thought popular music sounded like noise made by pounding on tin pans! Whatever the reason, the name has stayed, but now it refers to the entire pop music industry. "I wonder what kind of music **Tin Pan Alley** will come up with next year?" Bianca asked.

　　許多年前，紐約市有一地區集中了流行音樂創作人和發行人的辦事處，叫做 "Tin Pan Alley"，直譯為 "錫鍋小巷"。也許是有人認為流行音樂聽來像是敲打錫鍋發出來的噪音的緣故。今天，"Tin Pan Alley" 是指流行音樂業。

To Beat The Band

Gee, Granny! You may not like rock and roll music, but that doesn't mean you should attack the rock group **to beat the band**! "But they have been playing **to beat the band**, and Grandpa is trying to take a nap," Granny cried. If this conversation seems confusing, simply remember that **to beat the band** means loud, with great force, or in a remarkable way. "Grandpa had been snoring **to beat the band** but that music woke him up," Granny complained.

　　"To beat the band" 原本形容某活動比樂隊 (band) 演奏的音樂更加喧鬧和響亮，後來意指喧噪地、猛烈地或驚人地。

Too Big For One's Breeches/Britches/Pants/Trousers

Breeches, britches, pants and trousers are all the same thing, and except in this idiom it is probably rare to hear anyone say breeches or britches these days. But what does this idiom mean? Well, it's a way of saying someone is overly ambitious or thinks too highly of himself/herself. "Teddy is being very conceited these days. If you ask me, he's getting **too big for his britches**," Angela complained.

Breeches、britches、pants 和 trousers 都指褲子。當我們形容某人 "too big for his breeches/britches/pants/trousers" 時，我們是指他自視過高。

The Tools Of One's Trade

There's nothing complicated about the meaning of this expression: **the tools of one's trade** are the things a person would use in his trade, activity, business or profession. It could be his tools, instruments, utensils, or other things. "Books are **the tools of my trade**," Professor Oxbridge said. "Plates, hoops, rings and bowling pins are **the tools of my trade**," the clown laughed.

Tools 是工具。Trade 是行業。"The tools of one's trade" 意指某人在他的行業裏所應用的裝備、工具、器具或其他物件。

To The Nth Degree

The adjective 'nth' describes a huge amount or an unspecified large number. In this expression, it means to an extent or to a degree so great that it can't be measured or weighed. "Sally says her new job satisfies her **to the nth degree**." "It's so hot today that I am trying **to the nth degree** to keep cool," Teddy said.

Nth 是形容詞，形容龐大的份量或未指定的大數目。"To the nth degree" 的意思是達到無可衡量的程度。

Turn One's Stomach

"How strange," Dr Gaff frowned. "It appears to me that your stomach is where your head ought to be! In fact, it looks like you are all stomach!" That **turned Henry's stomach**. He had paid a great deal of money to get a specialist's opinion, and Dr Gaff (the specialist) was looking at Henry's X-ray upside down! If something **turns your stomach**, it has made you feel angry or disgusted.

雖然 "turn one's stomach" 并非是 " 使人反胃 " ，但亦含有使人不悦的意思。因為它意指令人憤怒或反感。

Turn Someone Off

From what I can see, the program Masterson has been watching on television has **turned him off**. "A lot of these old movies **turn me off**," Masterson said. "Don't they **turn you off**?" When something **turns you off**, it bores or distresses you. Or it is something that does not excite your interest. "People who don't appreciate my old movies and great acting **turn me off**," Max scowled.

　　有開關掣的東西，是可以隨意開關的。例如，當電視節目的情節令人感到不愉快時，我們便會把電視機關掉 (turn off)。由此，"turn someone off" 比喻使某人發悶或厭煩。

Under Someone's Heel

"Put down my cup of tea, Archie, and stay where you are. And please don't make any noise. I want to read today's newspaper in peace," Annie said. Poor Archie, his dear wife sure has him **under her heel**. That is, Archie is under her power or control. She has command over him. "How times have changed," Archie thought. "In the first years of our marriage, I was sure I had Annie **under my heel**!"

　　看字面意思，"under someone's heel" 是"在某人的腳跟底下"，用以借喻在某人的勢力之下，或者被某人所控制。

Up In The Air (1)

Adam has just made his first parachute jump.
Whether he will make another one is a question
that is **up in the air** at this moment. In fact,
whether Adam will get down to earth without
hurting himself is something that is **up in the air**!
The idiom **up in the air** refers to something that is
undecided or uncertain. "At this moment, my
entire future is **up in the air**." Adam cried.

    Air 是空氣。"Up in the air" 形容計劃、決
定、前途等懸而未決。

Up In The Air (2)

Teddy is **up in the air** today. His Uncle Felix has agreed to increase his weekly allowance. Angela is with Teddy, and she is **up in the air**, too. "I am **up in the air** because Teddy has agreed to use some of his allowance to buy me an ice cream cone," she smiled. In this case, when someone is **up in the air** he or she is very happy. "I am **up in the air** being able to share my wealth with Angela," Teddy said.

　　當一個人高興的時候，會有一種 "up in the air" 的感覺。這并非指他被懸在半空中，而是形容他雀躍萬分。

Walk The Plank

In days of old, when pirates captured a ship at sea they sometimes forced its sailors to walk overboard to their deaths from a wide board known as a plank. That's the origin of **walk the plank**, and it now means to meet with doom or disaster. "My loving wife warned me I would **walk the plank** if I didn't get home in time for supper," Sidney said.

　　昔日，海盜處死俘虜的一種方法，是把俘虜蒙住眼睛，然後逼使他在一個伸出舷外的跳板上前進，直至掉落海中。這便是 "walk the plank" 的由來，意思是惹禍上身或遭遇不幸。

The Warp And Woof (Of Something)

In a weaving machine, yarn extending lengthwise is called the 'warp'. The yarn in the machine that is woven horizontally is called the 'woof'. These are the two basic elements of weaving, and that has led to **the warp and woof (of something)**, which means the important principles of something. "An open mind and a willingness to learn about others is **the warp and woof of** friendship," Charlie Frog croaked.

紡織機上的縱綫，稱為整經 warp；它的橫綫，則稱做緯綫 woof。它們都是紡織的基本物件，只要來回地縱橫交織，便紡成布料。由此，"the warp and woof (of something)" 引申為某事物的基本要素或主要成份。

Washed Up

When something is **washed up**, it is at an end. It is ruined. It's a failure. People, too, are **washed up** when they are failures. For example: "The Ga-Ga Company is **washed up**. It stopped selling goods last year." "Mike's girlfriend left him. Their romance is **washed up**." "If I don't pass my examinations, I fear I will be **washed up**!" Ted said.

"Washed up" 形容人或事業一敗塗地，甚至是被毀滅。

Watch Every Penny

King Rufus is extremely wealthy. "That's because I am exceedingly careful with my money. I **watch every penny**," His Majesty said. Whether you are a pauper or a prince, to **watch every penny** is to be cautious how you spend your money. "The kingdom is indeed fortunate," King Rufus grinned, "for our nice Queen **watches every penny**, too."

便士 (penny) 是面值最小的英國錢幣。如果一個人每一分每一文都不隨便亂花，我們可以用 "watch every penny" 來形容他，意謂他用錢的態度十分謹慎。

Watering Hole/Place

To animals on farms and in the wild, a **watering hole** or **watering place** is a place where water can be obtained. To humans, though, a **watering hole/place** is a bar, pub or nightclub where people gather to socialize and drink alcoholic beverages. "I'm especially fond of Pete's Place. It's my favorite **watering hole**. What's the name of your **watering place**?" Joseph asked.

　　對農場牲畜或野生動物來說，"watering hole/place" 是牠們的飲水處。人類的 "watering hole/place" 不但另有所指，而且還是很講究的。它是指人們聚在一起喝酒、交際的酒吧或夜總會。

Weigh Something Up

"Children are really difficult to please," Helen sighed. "Look at them! See how they're **weighing their chances up** to see how to get the biggest piece of cake!" Little Johnny, in fact, is already **weighing up** the possibility of getting a second piece. This idiom refers to judging one's chances of success or failure in a situation or an action.

"Weigh something up"，原指稱 (weigh) 東西的重量；引申開來，就解釋為衡量局勢或行動的成功率。

The Welcome Mat Is Out

A lot of homes have welcome mats at their front doors, and a lot of them say 'Welcome'. That has a lot to do with the origin of this idiom, and it means that a person is welcome to visit your home at any time. "Come over to see me sometime," Sandra smiled. "**The welcome mat is** always **out** for good friends like you."

　　許多房屋的門前都舖有歡迎 (welcome) 字眼的門墊 (mat)。由此，"the welcome mat is out" 就比喻歡迎某人隨時登門造訪。

Well-Heeled

There is no doubt in my mind that Mr Gotrocks is **well-heeled**. He lives in a huge house, he drives a big car, and he belongs to some of the most exclusive clubs in town. "That's quite true, and my beach club is so exclusive that I am the only member!" Mr Gotrocks said. To be **well-heeled** is to be very wealthy – and if you don't believe me, ask my friend Mr Gotrocks!

　　腰纏萬貫的人一般都是衣着光鮮的，穿在腳上的鞋子也很體面，絕不會把鞋子穿到鞋跟 (heel) 被磨損為止。故此，"well-heeled" 就用來形容非常富有的人。

Whoop It Up

A whoop (the word rhymes with loop) is a shout of
joy or a cry of delight. That's the reason people
celebrating in a loud and enthusiastic way are said
to be **whooping it up**. "We have just won a big new
contract to export our goods to South America!"
the boss cried. "Let's go out tonight and **whoop it
up** by having dinner and celebrating our success!"

在一些歡樂的場合裏，人們有時會高興得
發出喝彩聲 (whoop)。所以，"whoop it up" 就解
釋為狂歡作樂，尤其是指為慶祝而歡鬧。

Wipe The Grin/Smile Off Someone's Face

"Whenever I submit my work to the art gallery, the selection committee laughs," Robert frowned. "It's sad, but this painting should **wipe the grin off their faces**!" With those words, Robert put the finishing touches on his latest portrait. To **wipe the grin/smile off someone's face** is to cause someone to stop feeling overly confident or self-satisfied.

"Wipe the grin/smile off someone's face"，直譯為"抹去某人臉上的笑容"，借喻使某人不再過於自信或自滿。

A Witch Hunt

"Nights like this are ideal for us to go out to conduct **a witch hunt**," Agatha grinned. I don't know what Agatha and her kind go searching for on moonlit nights, for the **witch hunts** I'm familiar with are those in which people are persecuted for having views – often political – considered different or unpopular. "I know. That's why I'm out hunting," Agatha laughed.

　　"A witch hunt" 源自古時搜捕被誣告為女妖的婦女。今天給引申開來,指以莫須有的罪名進行的政治迫害,尤指迫害異己份子。

Work Like A Plowhorse/ Plough Horse

A race horse has fun running in circles at racetracks, but the fate of a plowhorse (sometimes spelled plough horse) is to spend his days working on a farm. "We plowhorses are assigned such unglamourous tasks as pulling wagons and plows," Horace said, "so from that, a person who **works like a plowhorse/plough horse** works long hours, and he usually works hard." "I **worked like a plowhorse** to see my business prosper," Willy said.

　　當賽馬的馬自由地在馬場上奔馳時，耕馬 (plowhorse 或 plough horse) 卻得日復一日，年復 一年地做着艱苦、粗重的農工。"Work like a plowhorse/plough horse"，就比喻人像牛馬一般 長時間地艱苦幹活兒或工作。

Work Up A Storm

In this idiom, a storm is a determined – and often prolonged – burst of physical activity. To **work up a storm** is to work in a rapid manner or in a forceful manner. Here are some examples: "Patty is **working up a storm** to get her house cleaned." "Marion will have to **work up a storm** if she expects to finish her work today." "I'm going to **work up a storm** to learn every idiom in this book!"

"Work up a storm" 是美加兩地的通俗語。Storm（暴風雨）比喻一股堅毅、持久的突發幹勁。所以，這句成語便解釋為以堅定的意志力去勤奮地工作。

Worn To A Frazzle

"I sure wish there was some way that I could say that I was worn out, physically tired, and emotionally exhausted!" Bea sighed. Cheer up, Bea, for I think you are in luck. Since the word 'frazzle' (it rhymes with dazzle) means to be fatigued or exhausted, why don't you tell people you are **worn to a frazzle**? If you do, that expression will explain exactly how you feel. "Thank you very much," Bea answered.

Frazzle 是疲憊不堪之意。"Worn to a frazzle" 形容人精疲力竭，或者心力交瘁。

The Year Dot

"Wow, how time flies!" Richard exclaimed as he and Jo welcomed in the New Year. "You are right, and it seems to me we have known each other since **the year dot**," Jo replied. "But what's really important is that we have been happy together since **the year dot**," Richard smiled. **The year dot** is an undetermined point in time. "It is a point in time so long ago that we don't even know when it was," Jo said.

Dot 指一個小點。如果我們以一個小點作為年月的開端，便可想像 "the year dot" 應該是很久以前的某一刻或某個日子。

You Can Bet Your Bottom Dollar

Wait, Fergus! Before you take Herbie's bottom dollar (that is, his last dollar) you should know that when a person uses this expression, he is saying he is absolutely certain or positively convinced about something. Fergus was confused. "Why should I want to know that?" he asked. "Because **you can bet your bottom dollar** that Herbie's dad will punish you if you insist on taking Herbie's money!"

"You can bet your bottom dollar" 源自賭博，賭徒抱著必贏的信心，把身上僅有的錢孤注一擲。由此，這句成語比喻對某事非常肯定，或者極有把握。